Published by Creative Education and
Creative Paperbacks
P.O. Box 227, Mankato, Minnesota 56002
Creative Education and Creative Paperbacks
are imprints of The Creative Company
www.thecreativecompany.us

Design by The Design Lab
Production by Chelsey Luther
Art direction by Rita Marshall
Printed in the United States of America

Photographs by Alamy (Arterra Picture Library,
blickwinkel, Buiten-Beeld, David Chapman, John
Gooday), Dreamstime (Isselee), Getty Images
(Arterra), iStockphoto (chris2766, Tariq_H), National
Geographic Creative (DESIGN PICS INC), Shutter-
stock (l i g h t p o e t, Betty Shelton)

Library of Congress Cataloging-in-Publication Data
Names: Riggs, Kate.
Title: Foxes / Kate Riggs.
Series: Amazing Animals.
Includes bibliographical references and index.
Summary: A basic exploration of the appearance,
behavior, and habitat of foxes, the widespread
members of the dog family. Also included is a story
from folklore explaining how foxes can outsmart other
animals.
Identifiers: ISBN 978-1-60818-878-9 (hardcover)
/ ISBN 978-1-62832-494-5 (pbk) / ISBN 978-1-
56660-930-2 (eBook)

This title has been submitted for CIP processing under
LCCN 2017937488.

CCSS: RI.1.1, 2, 4, 5, 6, 7; RI.2.2, 5, 6, 7, 10;
RI.3.1, 5, 7, 8; RF.1.1, 3, 4; RF.2.3, 4

First Edition HC 9 8 7 6 5 4 3 2 1
First Edition PBK 9 8 7 6 5 4 3 2 1

AMAZING ANIMALS

FOXES

BY KATE RIGGS

CREATIVE EDUCATION · CREATIVE PAPERBACKS

Foxes live around the world.
They are members of the dog family.
There are 12 kinds of "true foxes."

The red fox is the most widespread of any fox

Foxes have fur and bushy tails. Their ears point up. Their snouts are long and thin. Around the nose are many soft, black whiskers.

Whiskers help a fox feel when animals are moving nearby

Male foxes are bigger than females. The largest kind of fox is the red fox. It weighs 15 to 30 pounds (6.8–13.6 kg). Fennec foxes are the smallest. They weigh about 3.5 pounds (1.6 kg).

Foxes that live in cooler regions are usually larger in size

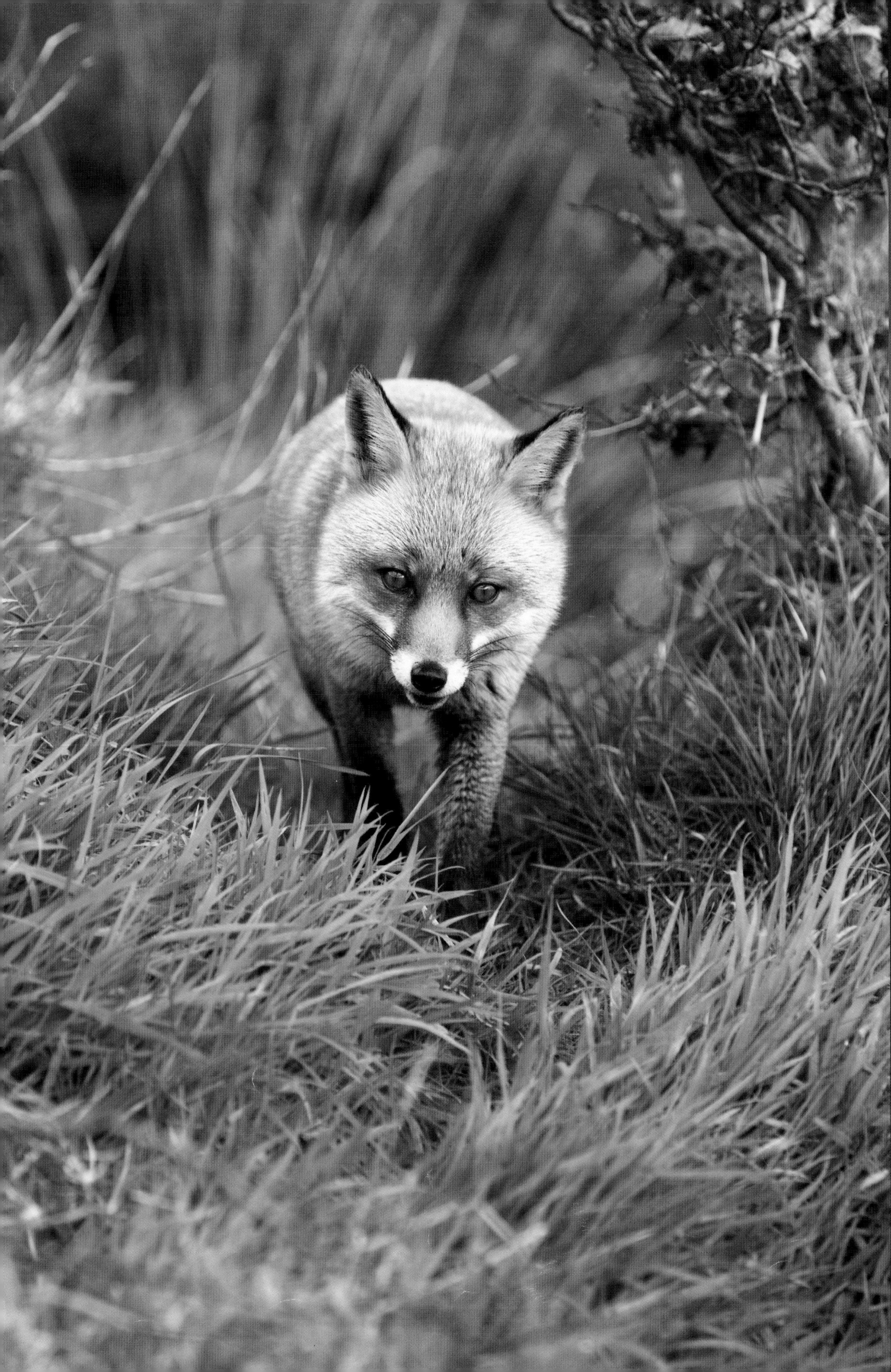

*Fennec foxes live in
Africa's Sahara Desert*

Some foxes live in cold, northern parts of the world. Some live in dry **deserts**. Kit, swift, and red foxes make their homes in North America.

deserts dry lands that receive little rain

Foxes usually eat meat. They hunt more at night than in the daytime. Some foxes also eat plants. They will eat eggs, worms, and beetles, too.

Foxes pounce on small animals when hunting

Kits' fur starts changing color after about three months

A mother fox typically has four to six **kits**. They stay in the **den** with her for the first two weeks. They start learning how to hunt after two months. Wild foxes usually live three to five years.

den a home that is hidden, like an underground space

kits baby foxes

Most foxes share a **home range**. But the red fox lives alone. Foxes sleep outside or in a den. There are many dens inside a home range.

home range an area of land where an animal finds food and spends its time

A fox goes around its home range. It marks the borders so that other foxes know who lives there. It hunts by itself. It runs fast to chase **prey**. A red fox's top speed is 30 miles (48.3 km) per hour.

prey animals that are killed and eaten by other animals

Quick foxes can be seen near towns and farms. They can be kept in zoos for many years. It can be exciting to hear a fox "scream" or howl!

Foxes in the same family group like to play-fight

A *Fox Story*

How did a fox trick a sea monster? Long ago, people believed in a snakelike monster that ruled the seas. The monster was angry with Fox. Fox had stayed on land instead of becoming a fish. The monster sent Catfish to get Fox. But Fox found out that the monster really wanted to eat Fox's heart! Fox tricked Catfish into returning to land. Catfish still hides near the bank. And Fox stays far away from the shore.

Read More

Green, Emily. *Foxes*. Minneapolis: Bellwether Media, 2011.

Read, Tracy C. *Exploring the World of Foxes*. Buffalo, N.Y.: Firefly Books, 2010.

Websites

Enchanted Learning: Foxes
http://www.enchantedlearning.com/subjects/mammals/fox/Foxprintout.shtml
This site has fox facts and a red fox picture to color.

National Geographic Kids: Fennec Fox
http://kids.nationalgeographic.com/animals/fennec-fox/#fennec-fox-hole.jpg
Learn more about the world's smallest fox.

Note: Every effort has been made to ensure that the websites listed above are suitable for children, that they have educational value, and that they contain no inappropriate material. However, because of the nature of the Internet, it is impossible to guarantee that these sites will remain active indefinitely or that their contents will not be altered.